ANIMALS ANIMALS ANIMALS

ALSO SPONSORED BY THE CARTOONISTS GUILD

The Art in Cartooning

ANIMALS

A COLLECTION OF GREAT ANIMAL CARTOONS

ANIMALS

EDITED BY

GEORGE BOOTH, GAHAN WILSON AND RON WOLIN

FOR THE CARTOONISTS GUILD

ANIMALS

HARPER & ROW, PUBLISHERS
New York, Hagerstown, San Francisco, London

Jacket/cover illustration credits (in rows, left to right, starting at upper left):

First row: pterodactyl, Michael ffolkes, p. 202; cat, A. B. Frost, p. 185. Second row: cat, A. B. Frost, p. 185; storks, Frank Modell, p. 38; dog, Arnold Roth, p. 26; ducks, Arnold Roth, p. 26. Third row: dog, Arnold Roth, p. 225; fish, Robert Brandreth, p. 81; hippo, Michael Maslin, p. 48; dog, John Dempsey, p. 209. Fourth row: cat, A. B. Frost, p. 185; monkey, Herb Brammeier, Jr., p. 229. Fifth row: dog, James Thurber, p. 18; frog, S. Gross, p. 108; dog, Arnold Roth, p. 225; dog, R. O. Blechman, p. 93; hippo, Charles Barsotti, p. 49; dog, George Booth, p. 52.

Back panel drawing by Jack Ziegler, p. 69.

ANIMALS, ANIMALS, ANIMALS. Copyright © 1979 by The Cartoonists Guild, Inc. All rights reserved. Printed in the United States of America. No part of this book may be used or reproduced in any manner whatsoever without written permission except in the case of brief quotations embodied in critical articles and reviews. For information address Harper & Row, Publishers, Inc., 10 East 53rd Street, New York, N.Y. 10022. Published simultaneously in Canada by Fitzhenry & Whiteside Limited, Toronto.

FIRST EDITION

Library of Congress Cataloging in Publication Data
Main entry under title:
    Animals, animals, animals.
    1. Animals—Caricatures and cartoons. 2. American wit and humor, Pictorial. I. Booth, George, 1926–   II. Wilson, Gahan. III. Wolin, Ron. IV. Cartoonists Guild.
NC1426.A5 1979   741.5'973   79–1653
ISBN 0–06–010429–5

79 80 81 82 83 10 9 8 7 6 5 4 3 2 1

ANIMALS ANIMALS ANIMALS

ALDEN ERIKSON

1

CHARLES SAXON

"Lily is the child. Violet is the dog."

BILL WOODMAN

FRANK MODELL

"How many times must I tell you? Stoop!"

T. S. SULLIVANT

The Camouflaged Steed: I'VE OFTEN HEARD OF THE HORRORS OF WAR,
BUT I NEVER EXPECTED TO BE ONE.

GEORGE BOOTH

WHITNEY DARROW, JR.

"Give up?"

Sauterne

Miss your tern

Western

FROM "THE BOOK OF TERNS"

Dramatic tern

A tern for the better
A tern for the worse

No stone left unterned

DRAWINGS BY MICHAEL C. WITTE

PETER ARNO

"If I were only twenty years younger and had my teeth!"

"Everybody hang on real tight in case he starts with a sudden jerk!"

CHARLES SCHULZ

ELDON DEDINI

"He knew too much."

R. O. BLECHMAN

FRANK MODELL

"Just who the hell do you think you're fooling?"

JOHN CALDWELL

11

ROBERT WEBER

"That dog is their whole life."

AL ROSS

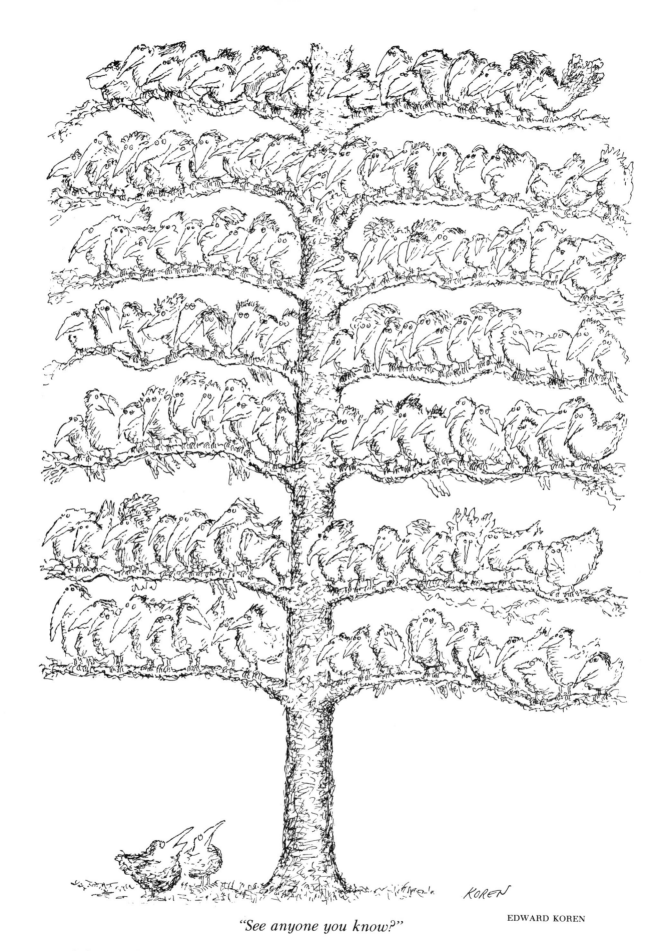

"See anyone you know?"

EDWARD KOREN

NOEL FORD

"It's amazing—no matter how much we encroach, the wildlife adapts."

MICHAEL MASLIN

"Well, it's all they ever gave us."

Richter

MISCHA RICHTER

THE HOUND AND THE GUN

JAMES THURBER

JAMES THURBER

"What have you done with Dr. Millmoss?"

CARL ROSE

"I'm afraid I haven't been much help to you, Miss. I'm awfully sorry."

BERNARD SCHOENBAUM

MICHAEL FFOLKES

"If you're not safe in the Empire State Building,
where <u>are</u> you going to be safe?"

ANTHONY TABER

M. K. BROWN

VIRGIL PARTCH

"You seldom see real alligator shoes these days."

ARNIE LEVIN

VIRGIL PARTCH

"Dear, is this our barrel full of monkeys?"

ARNIE LEVIN

A SHAGLESS DOG STORY
starring JULIUS the WONDER DOG... (he makes you wonder...)

ARNOLD ROTH

RICHARD RICE

JACK ZIEGLER

"Psst. Hey, mister. I got a message for your mayor. Tell him there's a plague of frogs camped just off Astoria in Queens. Tell him to cough up ten thousand gallons of flies or he won't even begin to know the meaning of the word trouble."

GAHAN WILSON

"But surely it must have occurred to you that the wide differences in your backgrounds would make your marriage more than ordinarily difficult."

DAVID SIPRESS

DAV HOLLE

"Tonight, how about something kinky for a change?"

JAMES THURBER

"You said a moment ago that everybody you look at seems to be a rabbit.
Now just what do you mean by that, Mrs. Sprague?"

J. B. HANDELSMAN

WILLIAM STEIG

"Nobody here seems to know how I can get back on Route 22."

JOSEPH FARRIS

"Any politician say anything worth parroting?"

PHIL INTERLANDI

PETER ARNO

"*He may be a fine veterinarian, but we're going to get some funny looks.*"

33

ELDON DEDINI

"Is it sundown already?"

BARNEY TOBEY

"The Graysons are on vacation in Europe. I'm the sitter."

MORT TEMES

"That's very good . . . only I said, 'Sit!'"

ORLANDO BUSINO

"There was nothing we could do about it. He has Blue Cross."

JACK MARKOW

"Are you sure it's your college song?"

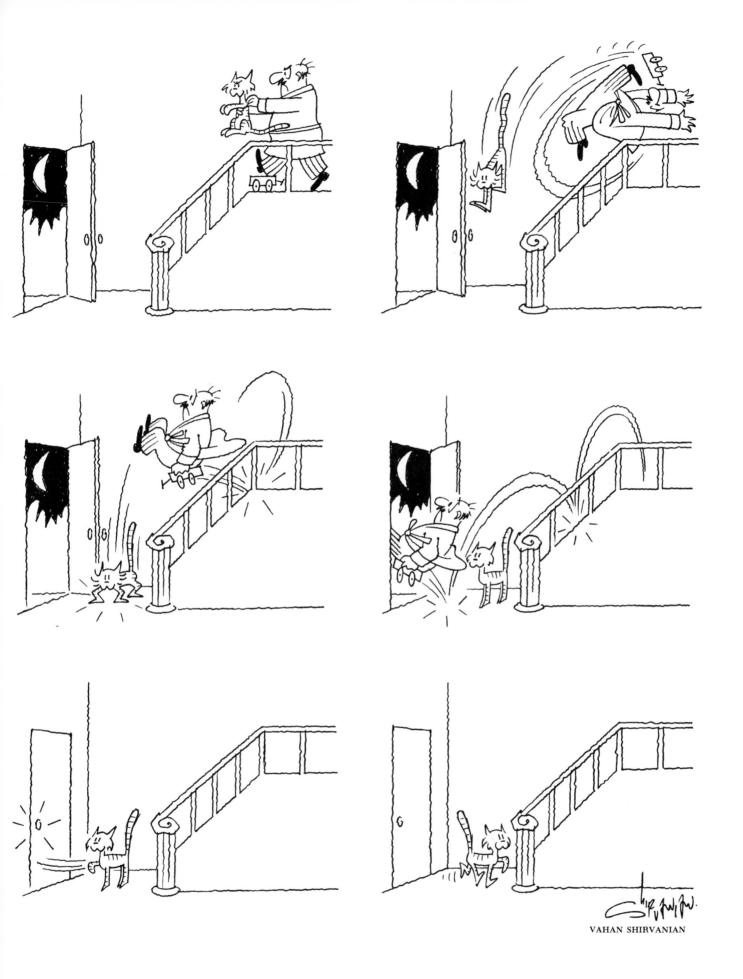

VAHAN SHIRVANIAN

H. T. WEBSTER

FRANK MODELL

ROBERT DAY

"You're sure she's got a friend?"

MARVIN TANNENBERG

LOU MYERS

GEORGE PRICE

"Lord, what a day!"

GAHAN WILSON

BILL TIDY

"Look out, it's . . . God, I'm awful with names!"

S. GROSS

43

WILLIAM STEIG

"Sure-footed little beasts, aren't they?"

GAHAN WILSON

*"Do you ever catch yourself wondering if all this
is only part of some crazy experiment?"*

ROBERT WEBER

"My God! Webbed feet!"

CHRISTIANSON

DAVID CHRISTIANSON

MICHAEL MASLIN

"Well, I can't seem to get through to them."

MARVIN TANNENBERG

"Well, if you didn't get so excited all the time,
your pearl wouldn't bother you!"

"Oh, you have teeth, too."

DEAF CATS TRYING TO FOLLOW A DUBBED FILM

BILL WOODMAN

BORIS DRUCKER

"Why don't they thin their own damned herd?"

VAHAN SHIRVANIAN

"You never know what you can do until you try!"

BOOTH

GEORGE BOOTH

*"There is very little heat in the luggage compartment and no air
conditioning at all, so stand up straight and stop licking your nose!"*

JAMES STEVENSON

STEVENSON

"As I understand it, they are seeking the poetry of solitude and communion with nature."

WILLIAM STEIG

53

ROBERT BRANDRETH

ELDON DEDINI

J. B. HANDELSMAN

"We younger fleas demand a bigger say in the running of this dog."

"Did you ever have a beautiful thought and you just couldn't find the words to express it?"

"Symbiotic relationship, my eye! The rent is due!"

WOODMAN

BILL WOODMAN

RICHARD RICE

"Don't blame me—you're the one who wanted a pointer!"

JOHN JONIK

JACK ZIEGLER

JARED LEE

"I hit a birdie!"

DOG OVERZEALOUSLY GUARDING A PIECE OF JUNK MAIL

JOHN S. P. WALKER

S. GROSS

HERB BRAMMEIER, JR.

"The herd will have to thunder without me—I have a splitting headache."

ARNOLD ROTH

61

ROWLAND B. WILSON

"O.K., everybody. Take five."

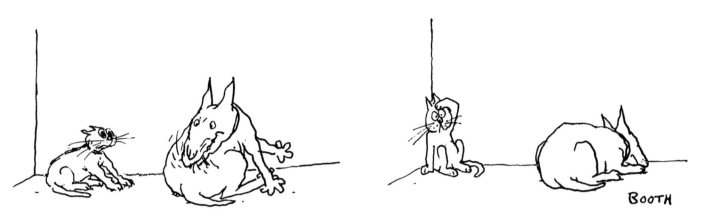

GEORGE BOOTH

WARREN MILLER

MORT TEMES

"Hold it, Tomkins."

INTERNATIONAL POLO WILL

GARDNER REA

"I'd say the front one is Edwards. He was always a little quicker on his feet than Davidson."

SHALL WE CANTER OVER TO THE WASH-STAND FOR A SHAMPOO?

MARY, WHEN YOU FINISH MASHING THE POTATOES, GALLOP OVER TO THE STOVE AND SEE IF THE TRIPE IS COOKED

BARBER SHOP POLO WOULD HELP THE BARBERS DEVELOP A LITTLE MORE ACCURACY THAN THEY HAVE NOW.

KITCHEN POLO WOULD MAKES THINGS INTERESTING FOR THE COOK.

RUBE GOLDBERG

HAVE US DOING EVERYTHING ON HORSEBACK

65

CHARLES ADDAMS

DON OREHEK

"Let's all wait for an open convertible."

ELDON DEDINI

"I'll go for help. And whatever you do, don't stop painting."

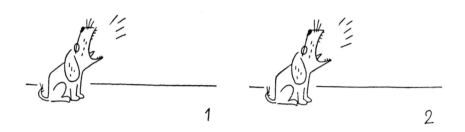

1

2

3

4

TON SMITS

JACK ZIEGLER

"Hello? Beasts of the Field? This is Lou, over in Birds of the Air.
Anything funny going on at your end?"

JOSEPH FARRIS

"*What a relief! We were afraid your form of life would be vastly different than ours!*"

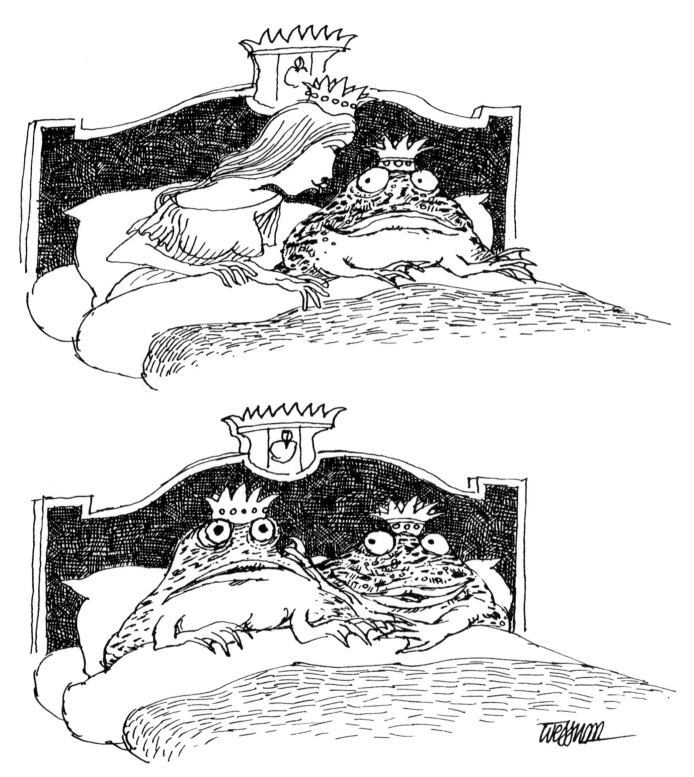

JAN VAN WESSUM

PETER STEINER

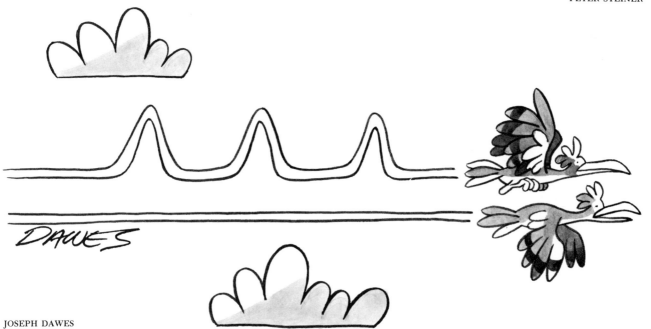

JOSEPH DAWES

"Well, if you wouldn't bolt your food you wouldn't have hiccups!"

MAL HANCOCK

"Offhand, I'd say he's part pointer and part setter."

DEAN VIETOR

"I know this sounds crazy, but my feet are cold."

MICHAEL MASLIN

"Don't give me those innocent looks. It sounded like a herd of elephants down here."

E. W. KEMBLE

A LITTLE CELEBRATION.

THE NEWS OF PARKER'S NOMINATION HAS JUST REACHED FROGVILLE.

WILLIAM STEIG

ROBERT KRAUS

"And now take this one here, I— Oh, good heavens!"

BRUCE COCHRAN

"You mustn't get upset when the other birds call you a turkey.
You <u>are</u> a turkey."

PETER ARNO

"I wonder what they did before we got here."

THE ACID TEST
FOR HUNGER

H. T. WEBSTER

COMING SOON ANOTHER CONDOMINIUM

DAVE HARBAUGH

ROBERT BRANDRETH

CLEM SCALZITTI

FRANK MODELL

"Don't tell me you have bad news, too."

JOHN GALLAGHER

VAHAN SHIRVANIAN

MIKE TWOHY

SAM COBEAN

"Aw, nuts! Why don't you grow up?"

WILLIAM HOEST

"I don't care if your name is Goldilocks—get the
hell out before my wife comes home."

WHITNEY DARROW, JR.

*"There's a character in this town I'd like to catch up with—a snub-nosed,
freckle-faced, barefooted little upstart in blue denims, goddam handy with
a slingshot. I guess he'd be about sixty now."*

SYVERSON

HENRY SYVERSON

ALEX NOEL WATSON

"Of course, all their reports about me have been greatly exaggerated."

ORLANDO BUSINO

"It started with him simply bringing me my slippers at home."

MORT GERBERG

"Protocol or no, if he doesn't stop talking soon, I'm gonna eat him."

MARVIN TANNENBERG

*"Oh, come now—you don't seriously expect us
to believe you depreciated over five thousand
shovels last year?"*

CHARLES ADDAMS   ©1952 The New Yorker Magazine, Inc.

ROBERT WEBER

"If this is the high point of our day, then I say something is radically wrong."

JOHN GALLAGHER

"Why don't you hang out the window like other dogs?"

ANIMAL
HOSPITAL
←

WARREN MILLER

R. O. BLECHMAN

93

DAVE HARBAUGH

"My turn!"

MICHAEL DATER

*". . . Cloudy later in the day, with a forty percent chance
of the sky falling tomorrow night."*

STUART LEEDS

ANATOL KOVARSKY

95

RICHARD TAYLOR

"I just got damn well fed up with being formal all the time."

MATERNITY WARD

JAN VAN WESSUM

OTTO SOGLOW

EDWARD SOREL

DOUGLAS REDFERN

*"I liked it better when we were a family farm
instead of a corporation."*

ANATOL KOVARSKY

HERB BRAMMEIER, JR.

ROBERT BRANDRETH

JOHN BLAIR MOORE

DUCK!

"It's only the wind."

THE ALMOST HOUSE-TRAINED DOG

ARNOLD ROTH

BORIS DRUCKER

104

RICHARD DECKER

"*All this trouble for a couple of snapshots.*"

MICHAEL FFOLKES

"*No, it was Edith who ended up as shoes. Alice ended up as handbags.*"

BRUCE COCHRAN

"That's a terribly tacky uniform. You look like you've gained weight . . . My, how you've aged . . . I understand your brother is making a lot of money . . ."

ALEX NOEL WATSON

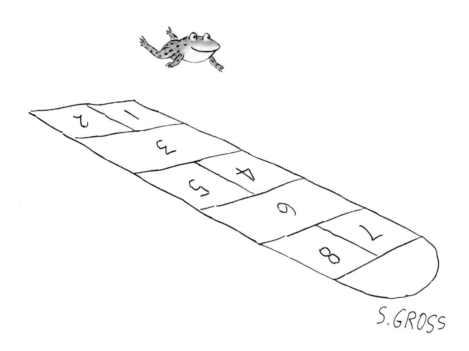

S. GROSS

ED ARNO

"I said, 'Never mind!' "

DAVID PASCAL

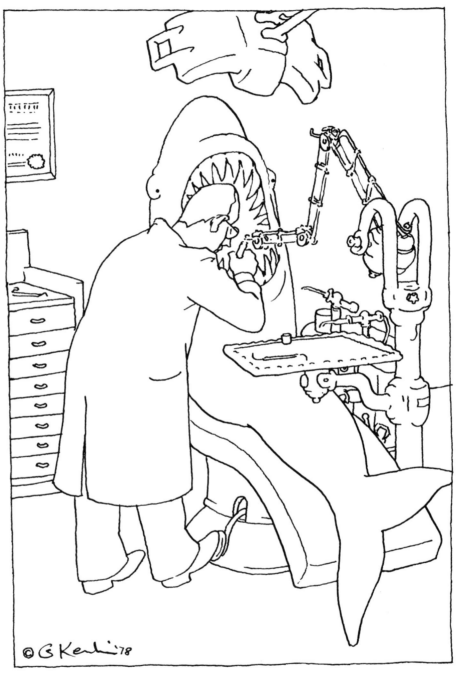

GILBERT KERLIN

MISCHA RICHTER

"Oh, it's you! I can't see a thing with this damn horn in front of my eyes!"

PHIL INTERLANDI

"It's damn big, whatever it is."

1)

2)

3)

ANATOL KOVARSKY

"Besides, it's so easy to make."

JESSICA STANLEY

*"Oh, he was rather a problem at first. But now
he just goes his way and we go ours."*

GARDNER REA

FROM EARLY SKETCH BOOKS

OF ABNER DEAN

BRONSON DANIELS, ORDERING TWO MORE, BEING MOCKED BY HIS DOG, LEONARD

JOHN S. P. WALKER

DAVID PASCAL

"I think that Jim's an absolute ass."

MAL HANCOCK

"I said, 'Don't you ever get tired of horsing around?'"

BERNARD SCHOENBAUM

©1975 The New Yorker Magazine, Inc.

"Oh, go away!"

GAHAN WILSON

BILL WOODMAN

"What's your dog's name?"

ALL YOU NEED TO JOIN THE GROWING CLUB OF MILD ANIMAL-HUNTERS IS A PAIR OF SCISSORS. THEY'RE ON THEIR WAY TO

BOOB McNUTT'S ARK

SO GRAB 'EM FOR YOUR COLLECTION AND PUT 'EM ON THE WALL

The LAMP-SHADE SPIDERS

The PROWLING SOOT-SOOTS

The BRUSH-FACED SKLUPS

SELECTIONS FROM "BOOB McNUTT'S ARK"

The CLOTHESPIN-HEADED CLOP-CLOPS

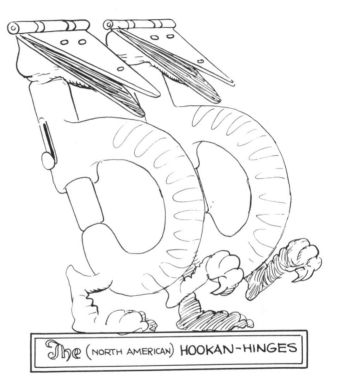

The (NORTH AMERICAN) HOOKAN-HINGES

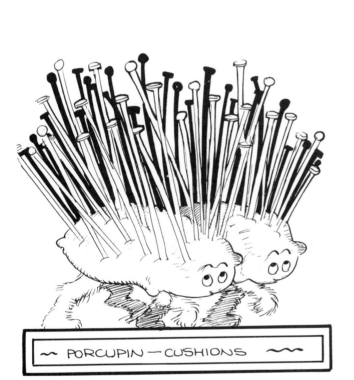

~ PORCUPIN—CUSHIONS ~

RUBE GOLDBERG

BY RUBE GOLDBERG

News Item

Only insects and bacteria will survive a thermo-nuclear war. The cockroach, a venerable and hardy species is most likely to take over the habitations of humans, scientist says.

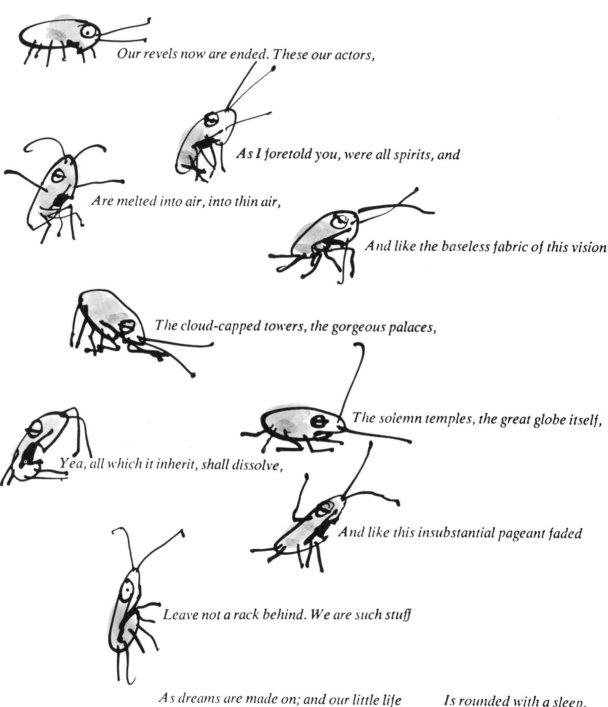

Our revels now are ended. These our actors,

As I foretold you, were all spirits, and

Are melted into air, into thin air,

And like the baseless fabric of this vision

The cloud-capped towers, the gorgeous palaces,

The solemn temples, the great globe itself,

Yea, all which it inherit, shall dissolve,

And like this insubstantial pageant faded

Leave not a rack behind. We are such stuff

As dreams are made on; and our little life   *Is rounded with a sleep.*

LOU MYERS

122

GEORGE BOOTH

"Say! The Purple Onion wants impersonators."

JAMES THURBER

*"For Heaven's sake, why
don't you go outdoors
and trace something?"*

DAVID PASCAL

ARNOLD ROTH

MARTY MURPHY

"You realize, Professor, if this turns out to be some kind of hoax, we'll be the laughingstock of the whole archeology community."

JAMES THURBER

"There go the most intelligent of all animals."

C.E.M.

DAVE HARBAUGH

"I was formerly a prince with a lot of liabilities.
Then my accountant introduced me to a witch with this
terrific tax shelter idea."

RICHARD TAYLOR

"The poor dear was one of the world's greatest big-game hunters until the Gaekwar of Baroda mistook him for a water buffalo."

CLARE BRIGGS

VAHAN SHIRVANIAN

*"Never mind how we found our way unerringly across miles
of ocean, river and stream to the spawning grounds. Spawn!"*

DAVID SIPRESS

"What's the matter, dear? . . . cat got your tongue?"

LEN HERMAN

*"I **know** it's hard to believe, but take a good look at their hands, the shape of their skulls, their upright walk—I tell you, we're descended from man!"*

WILLIAM HOEST

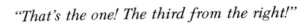

"That's the one! The third from the right!"

COCHRAN!

BRUCE COCHRAN

"I love your bulging eyes,
your wet, green skin,
your fat, puffy body . . ."

JOSEPH DAWES

*"Brontosaurus—thunder lizard—largest creature
ever to walk the land! Who the hell are you?"*

MORT GERBERG

"Ain't a fit night out for man and/or beast."

ANDRÉ FRANÇOIS

JOHN JONIK

ALDEN ERIKSON

BRUCE COCHRAN

"Predator meeting in the big clearing at midnight. Pass it on."

JOSEPH FARRIS

*"Don't let him scare you.
He's all hyperbole."*

DON DOUGHERTY

DEAN VIETOR

"President Carter this week opened negotiations for trade with the Far East."

MICHAEL MASLIN

"Oh, let me introduce you to my husband."

GEORGE PRICE

"I don't know what it is—I shot it one time when I had jungle fever."

138

EDWARD KOREN

"Your bell sounds lovely this evening."

CHARLES ADDAMS

"You certainly have a peculiar sense of humor."

CLARE BRIGGS

JERRY DUMAS

"Ferguson, I'd like a word with you."

1.

2.

3.

DICK OLDDEN

"Still up to your old tricks, eh?"

ORLANDO BUSINO

KRYSTYNA EDMONDSON

"I'm a hell of a lot more endangered than you are!"

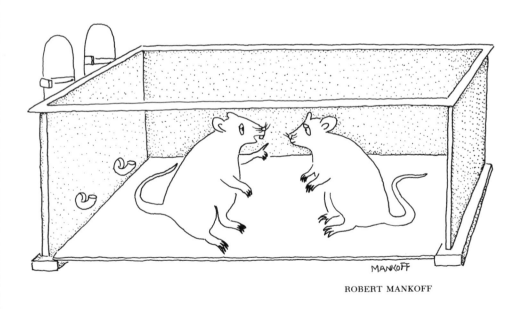

"My main fear used to be cats—now it's carcinogens."

COVER: "Horse Sense," *Life,* ca. 1920.

JOHN HELD, JR.

PETER PORGES

MICK STEVENS

"You do nice work . . ."

DEAN VIETOR

"If you hadn't lost the map we could have found our own way home."

MAL HANCOCK

"Ambrose, I thought jay walking was against the law!"

CALDWELL

JOHN CALDWELL

"No . . . I think you played very well. You misinterpreted my hissing."

ROLAND MICHAUD

"It's your divine <u>right</u> to bite!"

BARNEY TOBEY

*"Looking at us objectively, I'd say we were really
quite stunning creatures."*

ROBERT DAY

H. T. WEBSTER

SYVERSON

HENRY SYVERSON

T. S. SULLIVANT

MR. HO : *"I lost my balance as the street car started today and sat right in a monkey's lap."*

MRS. HO : *"Oh! I hope you apologized."*

MR. HO : *"No; it was too late, but I'm going to send a wreath."*

GEORGE PRICE

"Er—haven't you got one that's more resigned to its fate, so to speak?"

GEORGE BOOTH

"Was it a 'ittle putty tat?
'es it was. It was a putty!
Tum tum tum!
Tum on, pwetty putty,
tum det on Mommy's wap."

SAM COBEAN

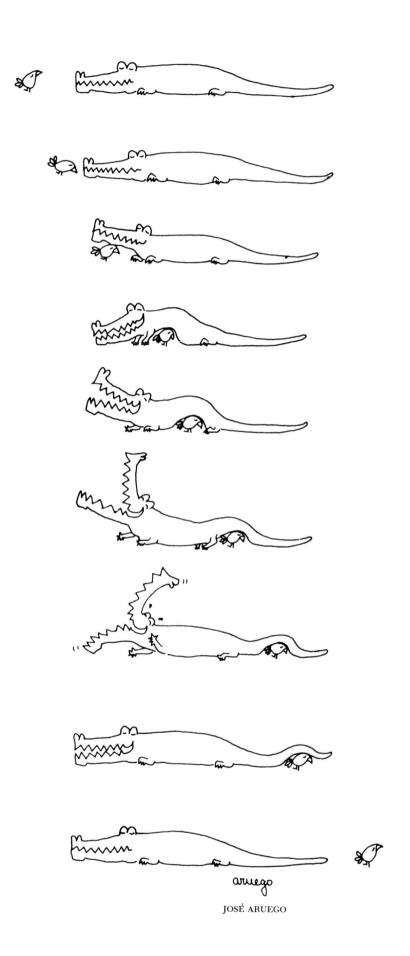

aruego

JOSÉ ARUEGO

DON DOUGHERTY

LEO CULLUM

RANDY GLASBERGEN

*"I got rid of the shell. It was hiding
all my erogenous zones."*

ANATOL KOVARSKY

ROLAND MICHAUD

*"Oh, the boys are doing well—one's with a cereal company
and the other's with a gasoline company."*

BILL WOODMAN

"Of course, right now it's only up and down, but we're working on the somersault."

REA IRVIN

DON OREHEK

"Are you sure he's hat-broken?"

MORT TEMES

"I enjoy spoiling him!"

160

ROBERT DAY

"Well, I don't know, I sort of had my heart set on a lion."

BILL MAUL

"Look, I know you're in there and I know you're a turkey."

JACK ZIEGLER

"Simply being a talking dog is no longer enough, George. These days one also has to be willing to take a stand on the issues."

"I was photographed this morning by an elderly white-haired lady in a salt-and-pepper tweed suit, bright scarlet scarf at the throat, blue porkpie hat with a multicolored feather on the left side, and green walking shoes with yellow laces."

JOHN RUGE

LARRY KATZMAN

"Your wife's name Mary?"

MARTY MURPHY

"I'm sorry to leave this way, but you know how long I've waited for an offer to do a porno flick . . ."

"You've got _worms,_ young fellow!"

"We never communicate anymore . . . we must be polarized."

KRYSTYNA EDMONDSON

"My son can't face us since he has failed to become the World's First Flying Baboon . . ."

LEO GAREL

"I understand that back in Roman days they tossed one in once in a while."

PETER STEINER

AL ROSS

"Hello, Ajax Office Furniture . . . ?"

BOOTH

GEORGE BOOTH

*"I want you to start thinking about someone <u>new</u> at our house. I want
you to start thinking good thoughts about a pussycat."*

MARVIN TANNENBERG

"And now, sir, perhaps you'd like to select a feather
to put in the band?"

MICK STEVENS

"No, no, Tippy . . . bad dog!"

ED ARNO

ED ARNO

"You only bring peace; I bring income-tax exemption!"

aruego

JOSÉ ARUEGO

DAVID PASCAL

T. S. SULLIVANT

HURDLE RACING BEFORE THE FLOOD

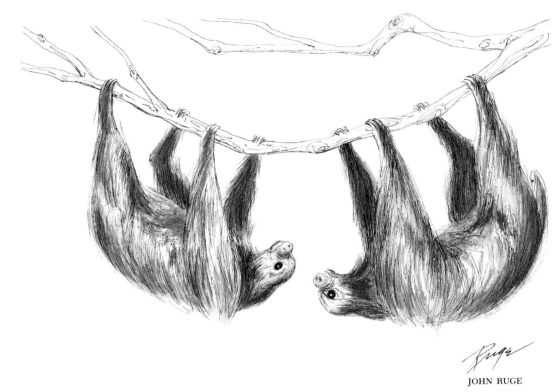

JOHN RUGE

"What I hate most in life is those damn squirrels running across my knuckles!"

PREPARING TO EAT CROW

JULIE FRANKEL & MICHAEL SCHEIER

FRANK MODELL

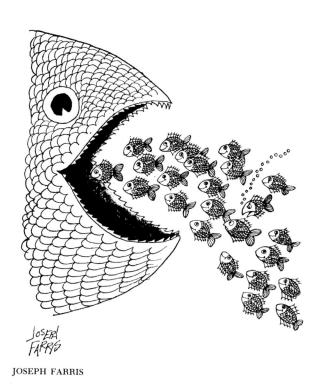

JOSEPH FARRIS

ED SZEPELAK

*"Quit complaining! He's the only
leader we've got!"*

*"Take two aspirins and call me back
in the spring."*

CLARE BRIGGS

GAHAN WILSON

"I think we've located the cause of that tie-up at Thirty-fourth Street and Fifth Avenue!"

LEO CULLUM

*"No, you're not disturbing me, Herb. I'm up
with the chickens this morning."*

ED NOFZIGER

"But you just had a drink last week!"

HENRY SYVERSON

IT'S JUST NOT HEALTHY TO HOLD BACK A SNEEZE, BENNY.

MY WHOLE LIFE FLASHED BEFORE MY EYES!

CRAIG LEGGETT

STEVE KELL

LO LINKERT

"Where did we go wrong?"

© 1976 by NEA, Inc.

CRAIG LEGGETT

DON DOUGHERTY

"Your chocolate moose, sir!"

"Yes, marm, all elephants take naturally to me. Now I'll hide these peanuts in my coat-tail pocket, and you just watch the circus."

She watches.

H. M. WILDER

"It was a delightful exhibition, sir, and would you mind doing it over again as soon as I bring my children around?"

EDWARD SOREL

Peace Offensive

JAMES STEVENSON

"Ah hah!"

DAVE HARBAUGH

*" . . . He says it gives him a new perspective on things,
but it sure is hard on the dog . . ."*

JOHN GALLAGHER

"Sometimes I wish he'd never shot the darn thing!"

The Fatal · Mistake·

A · Tale · of · a · Cat ·

A. B. FROST

SYD HOFF

"Maybe if the mailman brought <u>me</u> mail,
I wouldn't <u>want</u> to bite him."

JESSICA STANLEY

"Naturally, I used a nom de plume."

AL SWILLER

"Tarzan, Shmarzan! That's no way to talk to your mother!"

MISCHA RICHTER

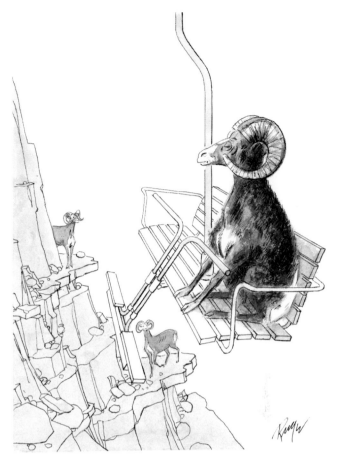

JOHN RUGE

ROLAND MICHAUD

"No, no, stupid, not that way . . ."

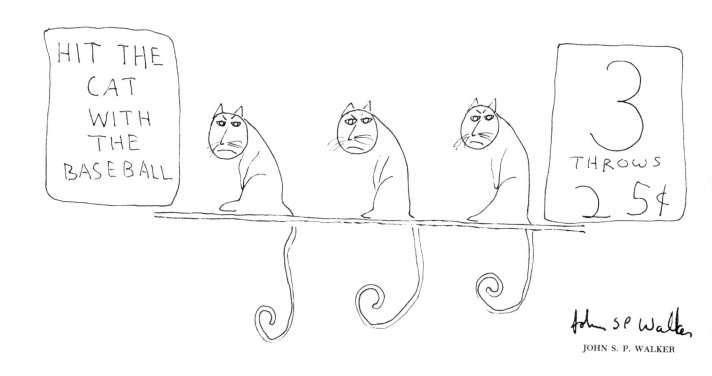

JOHN S. P. WALKER

LO LINKERT

MICHAEL MASLIN

"By the time I get him back in the house, he has to go out again."

DAVID PASCAL

"Goodbye, darling. I'm off to greener pastures."

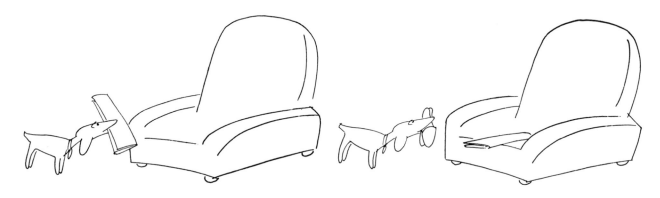

SERGIO ARAGONES

ED ARNO

CARL ROSE

*"With you, it's different. You've got talent,
courage, imagination, savoir-faire . . ."*

WILLIAM HOEST

*"Brace yourself, Grace. The doctor has discovered
the nature of my allergy."*

*"Have you tried a
muscle relaxant?"*

JOSEPH DAWES

196

MARTY MURPHY

"Frenchie, I've been thinkin' real serious about givin' up logging and gettin' me a job down in town."

BRUCE COCHRAN

"Perfect!! I'll mail your check when I get the insurance money!"

LEN HERMAN

"Soon the mating season will arrive and the tranquillity will be shattered by the territorial squabblings of camera crews from Jacques Cousteau, Walt Disney, and 'Animal Kingdom'!"

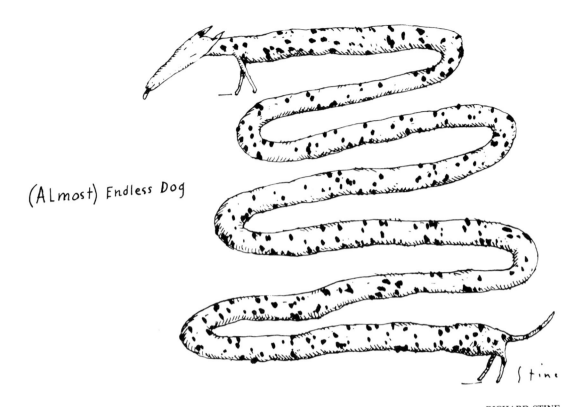

(Almost) Endless Dog

RICHARD STINE

Dog Face to
Face with the
Second Step

RICHARD STINE

199

"Quack."   "Moo."

"Quack."   "Gobble-gobble."   "Quack."   "Hee-haw."

"Quack."   "Baa."

"Quack."   "Oink."   "Quack."   "Quack."

"Quack!"

Richter

MISCHA RICHTER

Gall
N.Y.
©77

SREĆKO GALL

ffolkes

MICHAEL FFOLKES

"I'm Pterry, this is Ptom and this is Ptessa."

GEORGE PRICE

ED NOFZIGER

"All Clear!"

JACK MARKOW

SERGIO ARAGONES

MORT GERBERG

"Now you get right down there in the picture with the other lions. Don't you have any sense of pride?"

JOHN GALLAGHER

GEORGE PRICE

*"A magnificent fowl, madam. Notice how he looks you
straight in the eye."*

ED NOFZIGER

"My goodness, is that you? I thought all this was me!"

RICHARD DECKER

"You're not supposed to smile, Mr. Leary. The jungle-man is slowly tightening his viselike grip."

RANDY GLASBERGEN

*"Do you have any idea how embarrassing it is to sit on
an adopted egg for six weeks, only to find you've been
trying to hatch a pair of panty hose?"*

MARVIN TANNENBERG

"Oh, shut up and hibernate!"

JOHN DEMPSEY

"*Sorry, but I'm only qualified to take on people.*"

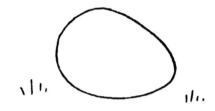

TON SMITS

BRILLIANT DOG TESTING AN INVENTION

JOHN S. P. WALKER

MICHAEL FFOLKES

"Every now and then, Gwendolyn, I get this feeling I'm going out with another chap."

ARNOLDO FRANCHIONI

*"You mean you don't recall talking to me
last night? . . . And I always thought you elephants
had such a good memory."*

ROLAND MICHAUD

"You just spread pollen. I spread dirt and disease."

J. B. HANDELSMAN

"You're right! It's the increasingly rare Pith-Helmeted
Rifle-Bearing Pink Explorer."

RICHARD DECKER

*"Certainly I get tired of it, but it's
the only thing I know."*

FRANK MODELL

1.)

2.)

3.)

Kovarsky

ANATOL KOVARSKY

215

ANTHONY TABER

MARTHA CAMPBELL

*"When I leave home, Mom's turning my
room into a briefcase."*

JARED LEE

JOHN BLAIR MOORE

WOODWIND QUINTET

ROWLAND B. WILSON

"Now if we could only lick the problem of pilferage."

"Well, Kendrick, still think I'm just an alarmist?"

JOSEPH DAWES

"Yep. Looks like a rough winter."

JON BULLER

JULIE FRANKEL & MICHAEL SCHEIER

JULIE FRANKEL & MICHAEL SCHEIER

CHARLES RODRIGUES

GAHAN WILSON

T. S. SULLIVANT

"Have you ever tried mud for your complexion?"
"My dear, I've simply wallowed in it all my life and it's never done me a
bit of good."

Have a veterinarian check your dog and give it the necessary shots.

Give your dog proper food and drink.

Some dogs have worms.

No worms have dogs.

Make sure your dog exercises.

Give your dog lots of love and affection.

ARNOLD ROTH

CHARLES ADDAMS

"Oh, for goodness' sake, forget it, Beasley. Play another one."

JOSEPH FARRIS

*"And to think all these years he was only trying
to tell us he was friendly."*

GLENN BERNHARDT

LEO CULLUM

"It's his only trick."

HERB BRAMMEIER, JR.

"Now there's a species that could vanish for all *I* care."

HERB BRAMMEIER, JR.

"It gets harder and harder to find the real Africa."

ED NOFZIGER

*"You wouldn't believe it to look at him now, but he was the ugliest baby
I've ever seen."*

MICHAEL FFOLKES

"Nevermore! Nevermore! Is that all you can quoth?"

JOHN CALDWELL

230

LEO CULLUM

"For the finish, go through the hoop into the tail walk followed by a double flip in unison . . . and I probably shouldn't tell you this, but there's a scout from Marineland in the stands."

PETER ARNO

"What you really want is to marry the girl and settle down. But you can't, because you're a gorilla."

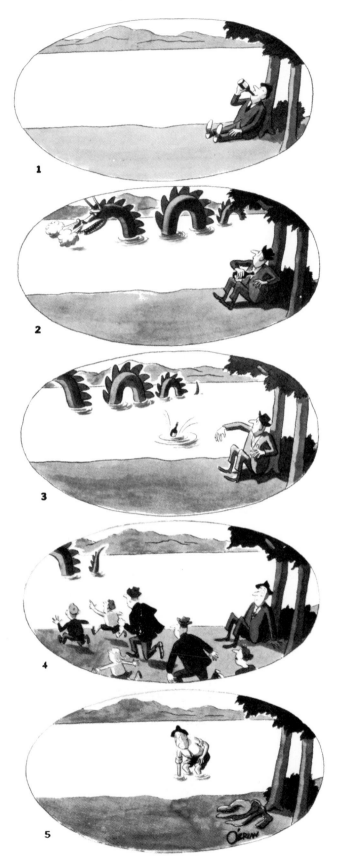

WILLIAM O'BRIAN

WHITNEY DARROW, JR.

"Now I see why everybody thinks they're extinct."

NURIT KARLIN

JAMES THURBER

ALDEN ERIKSON

"Madame, do I look like the type of man who would harm a penguin?"

WARREN MILLER

*"That's it, Duke! <u>Mmmm,</u> swell! But wag that tail
a little more, boy. Come on, damn it, let's see you
wag that tail!"*

JOHN CALDWELL

CHARLES ADDAMS

MIKE TWOHY

ACKNOWLEDGMENTS

The editors, Cartoonists Guild and Harper & Row wish to express their deepest thanks to all the artists and heirs whose kind cooperation has helped in the creation of *Animals Animals Animals.*

A special note of appreciation is deserved by Renée D. Pennington, who has provided enthusiastic and intelligent editorial assistance from the inception of this project.

We are indebted to the following copyright owners for permission to reprint cartoons owned by them:

Cartoon © 1976 *Advertising Age.*

Cartoons © 1975 and 1977 Sergio Aragones and E. C. Publications, Inc.

Cartoons from *The Book of Terns* by Peter Delacorte and Michael C. Witte. © 1978 Peter Delacorte and Michael C. Witte. Reprinted by permission of Penguin Books.

Cartoons © 1977 and 1978 *Diversion* magazine.

Cartoon by Alden Erickson excerpted from *1000 Jokes Magazine,* August 1966 issue. © 1966 Dell Publishing Co., Inc.

Cartoon © 1972 Mort Gerberg. From *Try It—You'll Like It!,* Dell Publishing Co., Inc.

Cartoons © 1973 and 1978 Hearst Corp. First published in *Cosmopolitan* magazine.

Cartoons © 1975 and 1977 Hearst Corp. First published in *Good Housekeeping.*

Cartoons © I.H.T. Corporation.

Cartoons © 1956 Anatol Kovarsky. From *Kovarsky's World,* Alfred A. Knopf, Inc.

Cartoon © 1967 National Wildlife Federation. First published in *National Wildlife* magazine.

Cartoons © 1976 NEA, Inc. First published in "Zoonies" syndicated panel by Craig Leggett.

Cartoons copyrighted by New Woman, Inc. are indicated throughout the book.

Cartoons copyrighted by the New Yorker Magazine, Inc. are indicated throughout the book.

Cartoon © 1975 David Pascal and Editions Jacques Glénat. From *Goofus.*

Cartoons © 1969, 1970, 1976 and 1977 *Punch.*

Cartoons © 1976 Arnold Roth. From *A Comick Book of Pets,* Charles Scribner's Sons.

Cartoon © 1977 The Saturday Evening Post Company.

Cartoons © 1976 Edward Sorel. First published in *The Village Voice.*

Cartoons © 1971 William Steig. From *Male/Female,* Farrar, Straus & Giroux, Inc.

Cartoons © 1975 and 1977 Richard Stine. From *Random Dogs,* Delacorte Press. A Delta Special.

Cartoons © 1943 James Thurber. © 1971 Helen W. Thurber and Rosemary Thurber Sauers. From *Men, Women and Dogs,* published by Harcourt Brace Jovanovich. Originally printed in *The New Yorker.*

Cartoon © 1955 James Thurber. From *Thurber's Dogs,* published by Simon & Schuster.

Cartoons copyrighted by Time Inc. are indicated throughout the book.

Cartoon © 1978 Gahan Wilson. From *. . . and then we'll get him!,* Richard Marek Publishers, Inc.

Cartoons © 1971 Gahan Wilson. From *I Paint What I See,* Simon & Schuster.

We particularly want to acknowledge the following heirs of ten great cartoonists for their assistance in making many wonderful drawings available to us: Patricia Arno Maxwell, Anne M. Cobean, Mrs. Rube Goldberg and George W. George, Mrs. John Held, Jr., Mrs. Rea Irvin, Barbara Rea Renwick, Mrs. Dorothy Rose, Anna Soglow, Maxine Taylor and Helen W. Thurber. Our book is so much the richer for the inclusion of this body of classic work.

Our sincere thanks go to the following artists, who are copyright owners of original drawings published for the first time in this collection: Jon Buller, John Caldwell, Bruce Cochran, Leo Cullum, Michael Dater, Abner Dean, Krystyna Edmonson, Julie Frankel and Michael Scheier, Srećko Gall, Dav Holle, John Jonik, Nurit Karlin, Steve Kell, Gilbert Kerlin, Anatol Kovarsky, Michael Maslin, Roland Michaud, John Blair Moore, Marty Murphy, David Pascal, Richard Rice, Ton Smits, Jessica Stanley, Mick Stevens, Dean Vietor, John S. P. Walker, and Alex Noel Watson.

Grateful acknowledgment is also made to the following publications in whose pages or through whose auspices many of the cartoons reprinted in this book first appeared: ABA Press, *Ag World, American Journal of Nursing, American Teacher, Argosy, Audubon* magazine, Bantam Books, *The Boston Phoenix, Boy's Life, Bulletin of the Atomic Scientists, Campus Life, Chevron USA, The Critic, Dude, Esquire, The Farmer, Harper's Weekly, Ladies' Home Journal, Maclean's, The Magazine of Fantasy & Science Fiction, Modern Medicine, National Enquirer, National Lampoon, Nebelspalter, The New York Times, Nugget, Pardon, Pets of the World, The Saturday Evening Post, Saturday Review, Sierra, The Sierra Club Bulletin, The Soho Weekly News,* and *The Washingtonian.*

Great care has been taken to trace the ownership of every cartoon selected and to make full acknowledgment for its use. If any permissions are omitted through error, necessary apologies and credits will be made.

INDEX